My Big Book of ADVENTURES

Words by Camilla de la Bédoyère

Miles Kelly

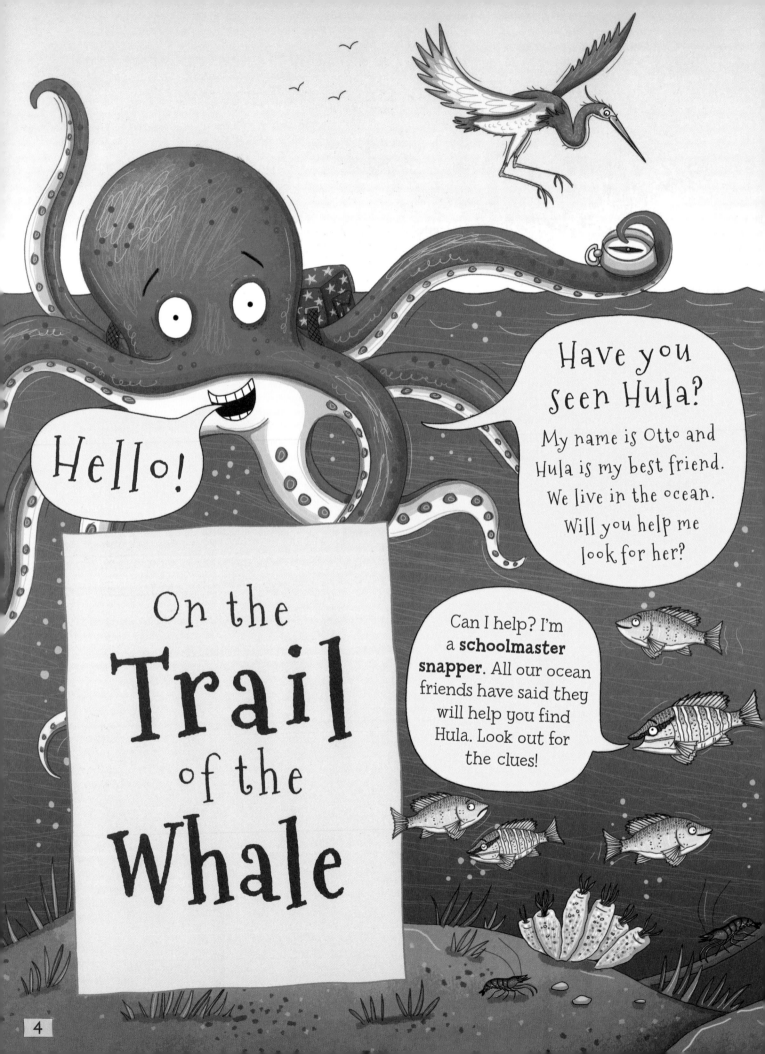

Hello!

On the Trail of the Whale

Have you seen Hula?
My name is Otto and Hula is my best friend. We live in the ocean. Will you help me look for her?

Can I help? I'm a **schoolmaster snapper**. All our ocean friends have said they will help you find Hula. Look out for the clues!

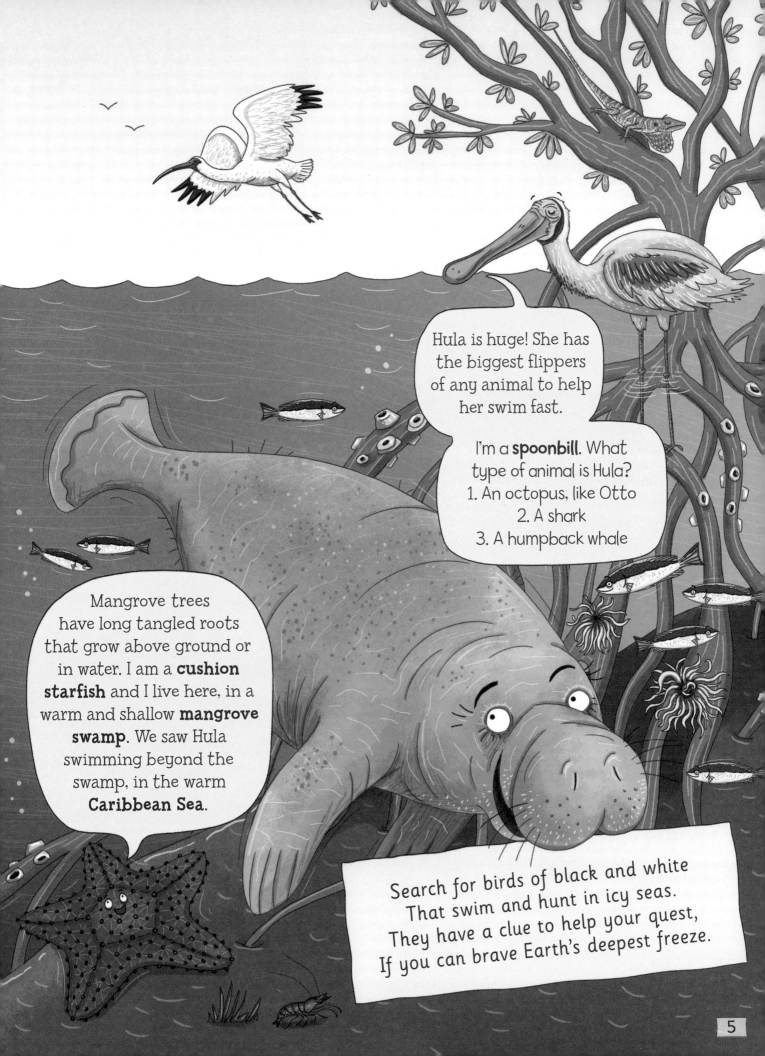

Hula is huge! She has the biggest flippers of any animal to help her swim fast.

I'm a **spoonbill**. What type of animal is Hula?
1. An octopus, like Otto
2. A shark
3. A humpback whale

Mangrove trees have long tangled roots that grow above ground or in water. I am a **cushion starfish** and I live here, in a warm and shallow **mangrove swamp**. We saw Hula swimming beyond the swamp, in the warm **Caribbean Sea**.

Search for birds of black and white
That swim and hunt in icy seas.
They have a clue to help your quest,
If you can brave Earth's deepest freeze.

SHARK SCHOOL

BLACKTIP REEF SHARK:
ALL FINS HAVE BLACK TIPS

WHITETIP REEF SHARK:
BROWN SKIN AND WHITE TIPS TO FINS

GREY REEF SHARK:
ALL FINS HAVE DARK TIPS,
EXCEPT THE DORSAL FIN*

* A shark's dorsal fin is the big
triangle-shaped fin on its back

You'll find Hula in the Black Sea.

This is a school for sharks! The blacktip reef shark has seen a whale. Follow her advice, and you might find Hula!

But which shark is which? Maybe the facts on the board will help me...

This part of the ocean is called the **Dark Zone** – no sunlight reaches it.

Oh no – that's not Hula. The blacktip reef shark got her whales confused!

The **Pacific Ocean** is the deepest ocean in the world – its deepest point is nearly 11 kilometres down! The pressure of water from above is so great that only special animals can live here – like me. I'm a giant spider crab.

Mind out – I'm fishing here! I'm a **double-crested cormorant**. We saw your friend — she sang us a lovely song, but now she's gone.

Baby fish like us live in a kelp forest. We can hide from big scary animals here.

We saw a whale and heard a whale,
She sang the sweetest song.
About the wondrous northern lights,
And ice bears, white and strong.

18

At night, temperatures in the Arctic are always below freezing and the sky flashes and glows with curtains of green and blue called the Northern Lights. We **reindeer** have thick woolly coats to keep us warm.

I'm a **narwhal** – famous for my long tusk. When you have found these three animals that are camouflaged in the snow you can turn the page:
Arctic fox
Snowy owl
Arctic hare

Follow me Otto, I'm an **orca**. I can hear lots of animals on the next page – maybe one of them knows where Hula has gone.

SWIMMING GALA

The race is about to **start**!

The letter on the speediest seal's back tells you which direction to go next – North, South, East or West. But which one is the fastest?

I'm a **walrus** by the way. See my tusks? They are teeth, and each one can grow to one metre long!

M

Seals can dive 4000 metres deep and stay underwater for up to one hour. It makes them tricky to catch, even for **orcas** like me and other top predators.

When seals swim really fast we hold our flippers against the sides of our bodies. Watch me! I can swim **6** metres in **12** seconds.

Some seals can swim at more than 30 kilometres an hour when chasing fish! I'm feeling fit – I can swim **6** metres in **6** seconds.

This is a **rocky seashore**!

These are my kids – **seahorse** dads look after our babies in a pouch on our tummies, until they grow big enough to swim on their own.

Hula stayed here for a while because she needed to rest. We **hermit crabs** live in seashells.

Puffins like me are easy to spot – we're so colourful. Some bottlenose dolphins live here too. I think one of them saw Hula.

The tide comes in, and goes out. We limpets get battered by waves, wind and rain, so we cling tightly to the rocks!

If you add the number of legs on one puffin to the number of legs on one crab, is the answer more or less than 10? I'm a conger eel – I don't have any legs!

23

We're just off the coast, in the **Atlantic Ocean**, and a harbour porpoise is swimming with some dolphins. He'll tell you the right way to go next. Don't listen to the dolphins — they'll send you the wrong way!

These dolphins all have a long snout, called a 'beak' and a curved top fin that helps them swim fast. Porpoises are usually smaller than dolphins, with a round head, no beak, and a top fin that is triangle-shaped.

I can grow more than 2 metres long. My baby is called a calf and it stays close to me. Hula is in the world's smallest ocean.

We talk to each other using clicks, whistles and songs.

I am a **dugong**. Like Hula, I am a mammal. That means I breathe in air, not in water. I give birth to my babies and feed them with milk.

Can you find any other ocean mammals in this book?

You've been on the trail of a whale
And a journey of more than a year.
You'll find your friend on the very next page,
But do you know why she is here?

You've been on an adventure,
Meeting creatures on the way,
Tick the boxes if you saw them,
When you finish, shout "Hooray!"

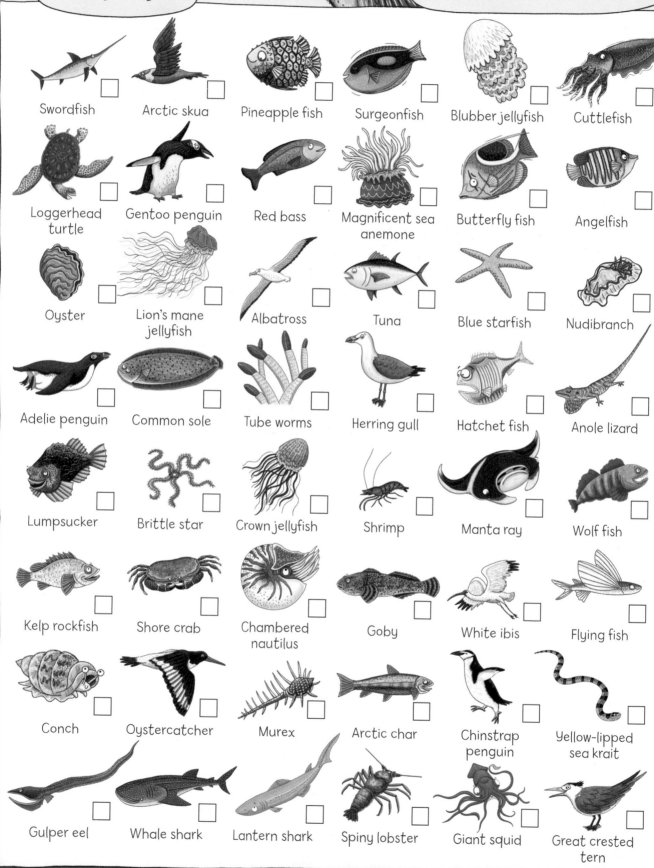

Swordfish ☐
Arctic skua ☐
Pineapple fish ☐
Surgeonfish ☐
Blubber jellyfish ☐
Cuttlefish ☐

Loggerhead turtle ☐
Gentoo penguin ☐
Red bass ☐
Magnificent sea anemone ☐
Butterfly fish ☐
Angelfish ☐

Oyster ☐
Lion's mane jellyfish ☐
Albatross ☐
Tuna ☐
Blue starfish ☐
Nudibranch ☐

Adelie penguin ☐
Common sole ☐
Tube worms ☐
Herring gull ☐
Hatchet fish ☐
Anole lizard ☐

Lumpsucker ☐
Brittle star ☐
Crown jellyfish ☐
Shrimp ☐
Manta ray ☐
Wolf fish ☐

Kelp rockfish ☐
Shore crab ☐
Chambered nautilus ☐
Goby ☐
White ibis ☐
Flying fish ☐

Conch ☐
Oystercatcher ☐
Murex ☐
Arctic char ☐
Chinstrap penguin ☐
Yellow-lipped sea krait ☐

Gulper eel ☐
Whale shark ☐
Lantern shark ☐
Spiny lobster ☐
Giant squid ☐
Great crested tern ☐

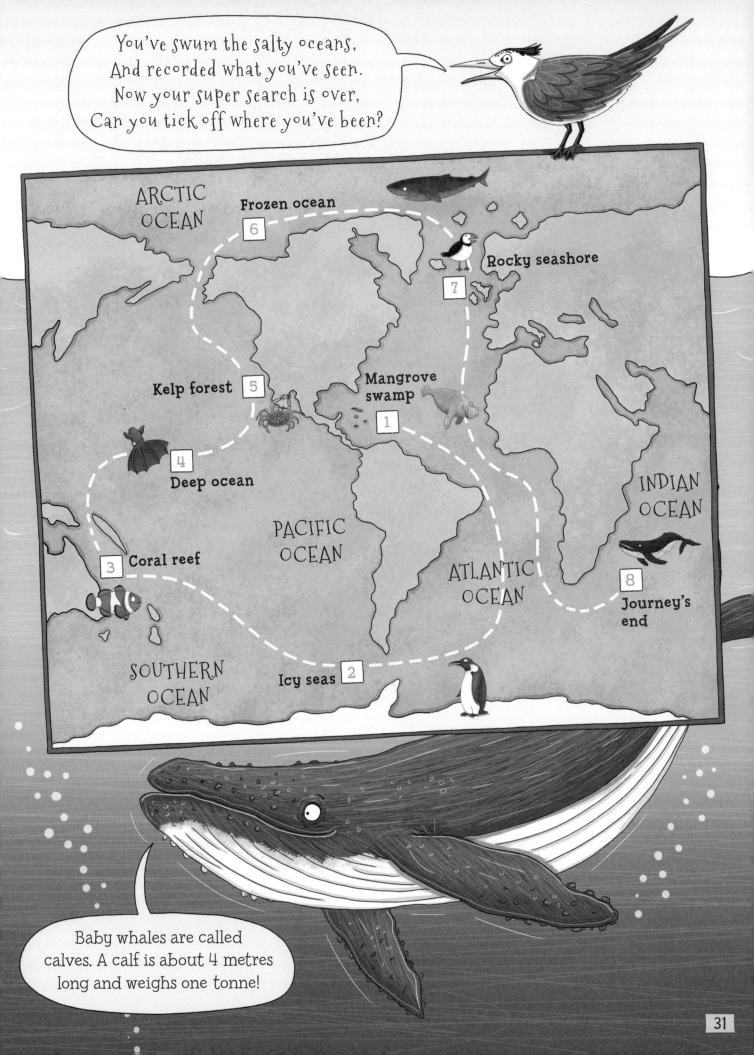

Hi **Suki**! We have a birthday present for our cousin Ping, but we can't find him.

Can you help us?

Where is the Bear?

33

Huge, strong grizzlies love a fishy feast. I'm sitting here because **lynxes** like me love to snack on any leftovers! Do you think I'm part of the dog family, or the cat family?

I'm a prickly **porcupine** and I'm covered in quills. I use them to defend myself from... big black bears! Follow that bear, Suki!

If Ping isn't by the river
Feasting on a fish or three,
Maybe he prefers the forest
And climbs up trees, like me?

We **sockeye salmon** are heading upriver to lay our eggs. Once hatched, our babies will swim back down river to the ocean. They will live there until they are old enough to lay eggs.

Help!

GRRRRR... go away! I'm not Ping, I'm a **grizzly bear** and I AM VERY BUSY!

There are thousands of us making this journey. It's called a migration. How many of us can you see?

37

We have bears here in the Californian **redwood forest**, Suki, but I've never met a bear called Ping.

If you're not Ping, who are you?

I'm an **American black bear**. I'm tearing bark off this tree so I can find juicy bugs hiding underneath!

If you match the animals to their descriptions you will reach an owl who may be able to help. I'm a **yellow-cheeked chipmunk**. I climb trees to find insects, seeds, leaves, nuts and flowers to eat. I live in a cosy burrow at the foot of this tree.

I'm striped to warn that I can sting.
My busy buzz is how I sing.
What am I?

Welcome to our **cloud forest** in the Andes mountains in Peru.

I'm a **jaguar**. We live high in the mountains, where the trees meet the clouds. It's damp, drizzly and foggy.

Are you Ping?

I am a **frog-eating snake**. I slip and slither silently through the trees, tasting the air with my long, forked tongue. My skin is covered in scales that help me to slide over branches.

No, my name is Specs and I'm a **spectacled bear**. I'm looking for ants to eat. Maybe Ping is a bear that eats leaves, not ants?

I'm a **tapir**. My baby has spots and stripes so he blends into his surroundings. Unscramble these letters to make a word that describes this survival tactic: CAFEGULOMA

Yawn! What's all the fuss about? Zzzzzz... I'm a sleepy little **Pacarana** and now you've all woken me up! I am nocturnal, which means I prefer to sleep during the day, and search for food at night... zzzzzzz.

It's time to hop across the sea,
Your present tight in hand,
To where a bear eats only leaves
In a dry and lonely land.

45

51

This is the tropical rainforest of **Borneo** – the third largest island in the world.

It's home to some incredible – and rare – animals, including **proboscis monkeys** like me.

A 'proboscis' is a nose, and look at the nose on him! I'm a **hornbill** and I've got a giant bill, or beak.

I am called a **sun bear** because of the pale fur on my chest – some people say it looks like a sunrise. My 20-centimetre-long tongue is perfect for scooping grubs and honey from bees' nests.

I'm a type of crocodile called a **false gharial**. I grow more than 3 metres long!

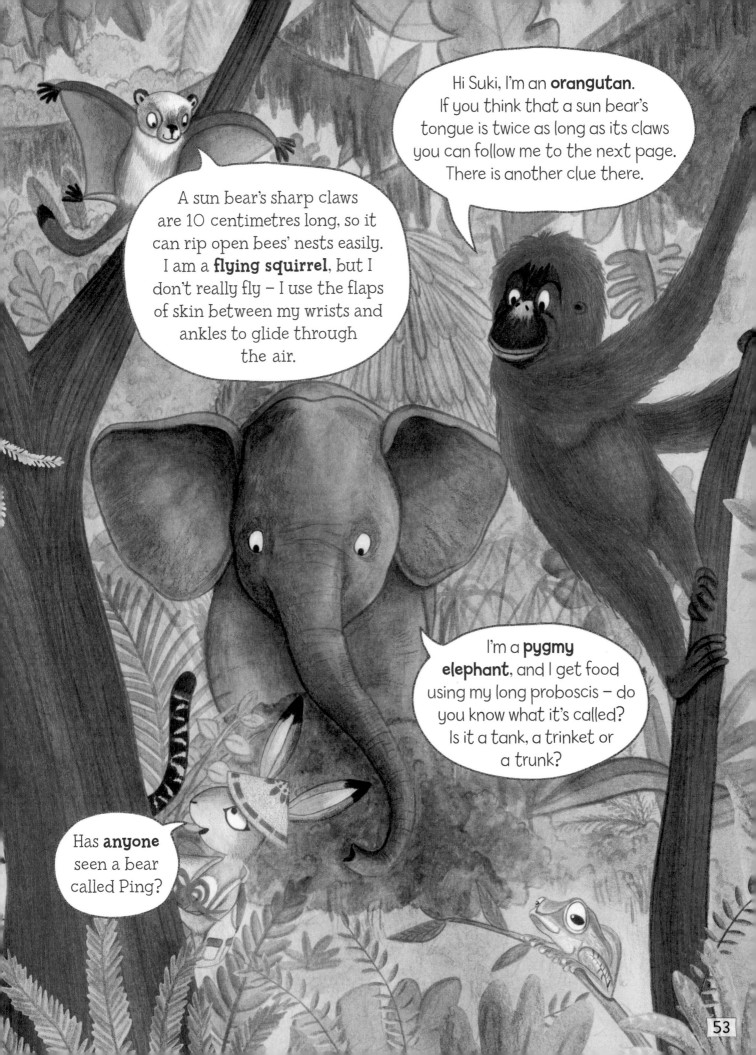

I'm helping my youngsters to learn about forests.

We **orangutans** are very smart apes. We love to learn new things, and mothers pass their knowledge on to their children.

Did you know that **sun bears**, like me, are the smallest bears? We are half the size of American black bears. That means that Ping is a type of bear that grows bigger than me.

COOL CONIFER FORESTS:
THE TREES HAVE NEEDLE-LIKE LEAVES
BEARS THAT LIVE HERE HIBERNATE IN THE WINTER.

WOODLAND:
COOLER AND DRIER THAN A RAINFOREST.
BROWN BEARS AND BLACK BEARS LIVE HERE.

BAMBOO FOREST:
WARM IN THE SUMMER, COLD IN WINTER.
PING LIVES HERE.

TROPICAL RAINFOREST:
HOT AND RAINY.
SUN BEARS LIVE HERE.

Suki has met polar bears, black bears, brown bears (including grizzlies), sun, sloth and moon bears. I think there is one type of bear she hasn't met yet. Can you guess what type of bear Ping might be?

These little ones are very playful, but they don't seem to be concentrating on their lesson! I think I've spotted a useful clue. Now I know where I'll find Ping!

You've been on an adventure,
Meeting creatures on the way,
Tick the boxes if you saw them,
When you finish, shout "Hooray!"

Rajah Brook's birdwing butterfly

Buzzard

Yellow-throated marten

Spangled drongo

Steller's jay

Walrus

Golden pheasant

Ermine

Borneo eared frog

Chamois

Mistletoe bird

Lace monitor

White-tailed eagle

Green-capped tanager

Mountain goat

Dark green fritillary butterfly

Arctic skua

King cobra

Glass frog

Ural owl

Spiny rat

Bornean bristlehead

Reindeer

Andean cock-of-the-rock

Ivory gull

Greater glider

Horned curassow

Clouded leopard

Sugar glider

Monitor lizard

Roe deer

Graceful tree frog

Geoffroy's cat

Arctic wolf

Northern spotted owl

Spotted nutcracker

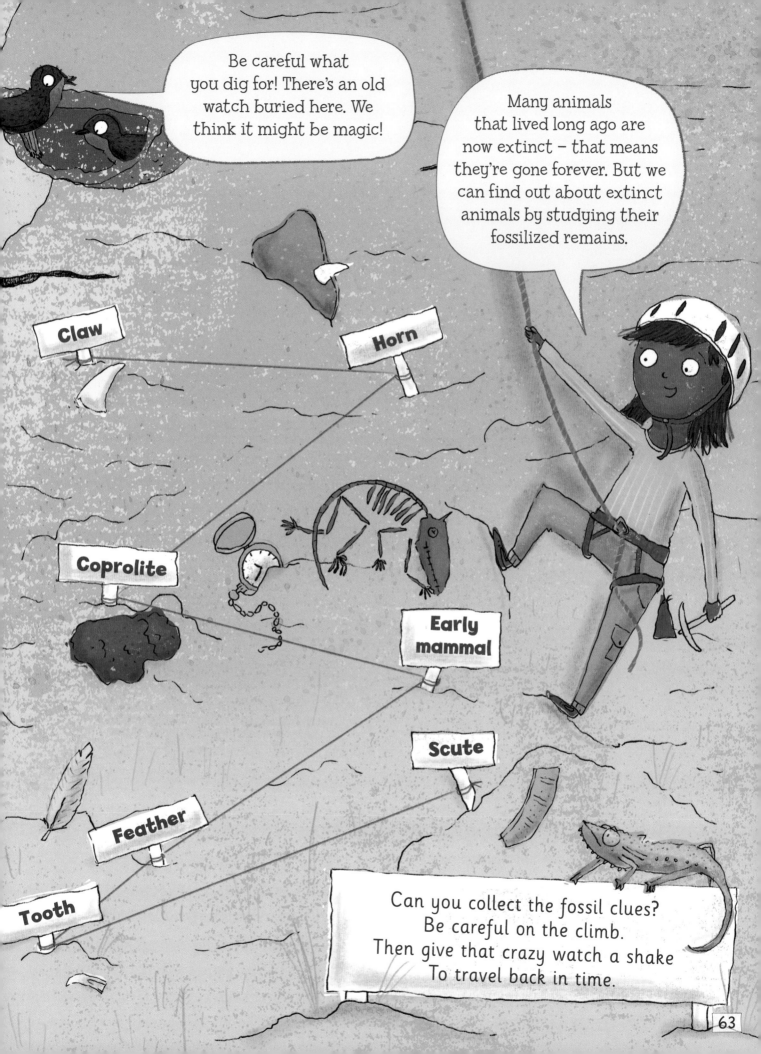

My name is **Dimorphodon**. From tip to tip, my wings measure 150 centimetres!

Most of us are flying reptiles, or pterosaurs – but one animal here is more bird-like than the rest! Find it, and follow its clue.

There are so many types of pterosaurs here – but the **Jurassic Period** is also when the first birds appeared.

Maybe this fossil feather will help us work out who can help us?

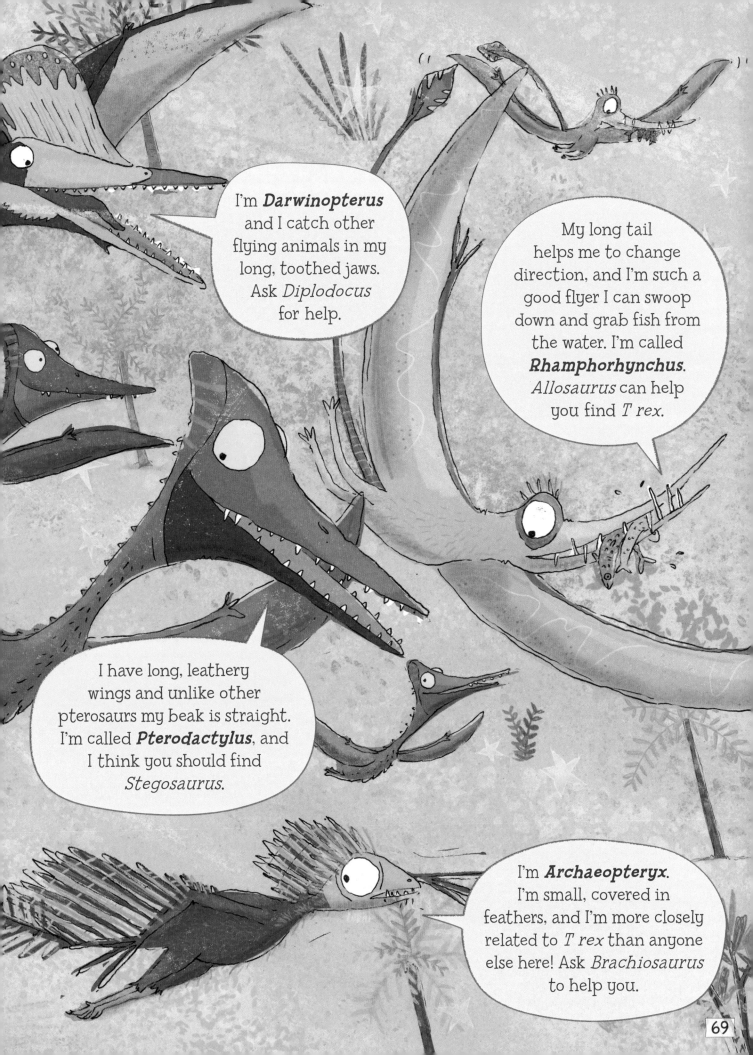

Welcome to the Cretaceous Period! I'm **Confuciusornis**.

In the Triassic Period, there was a single huge continent called Pangaea. Now it has split up into lots of lands, separated by oceans.

This fossil looks like **you**. Can you help us find *T rex*?

I'm a furry little mammal called **Eomaia**. I've never heard of *T rex* but *Confuciusornis* told us that she's seen lots of scary dinosaurs on the other side of the ocean.

Here in the Cretaceous Period, lots of dinosaurs have fuzzy feathers, like me – I'm **Sinosauropteryx**.

This is what I have learned about *T rex* so far...

• THIS HERBIVORE LOVED EATING LEAVES

• ITS HEAD WAS 150 CENTIMETRES LONG

• T REX HAD LITTLE ARMS AND TINY HANDS

• IT HAD 50 HUGE TEETH

Oh dear, Ava has only got three of these facts right. Do you know which one is wrong?

Flowers are growing all over the world now. Can you subtract the number of purple flowers from the number of white flowers?

Search the land or scour the skies, You'll find no *T rex* here. Nip across the sea to see The monsters that we fear.

Our fuzzy feathers aren't for flying. They keep us warm – and make us colourful too! I'm **Utahraptor**. The big claws on my second toes are 22 centimetres long.

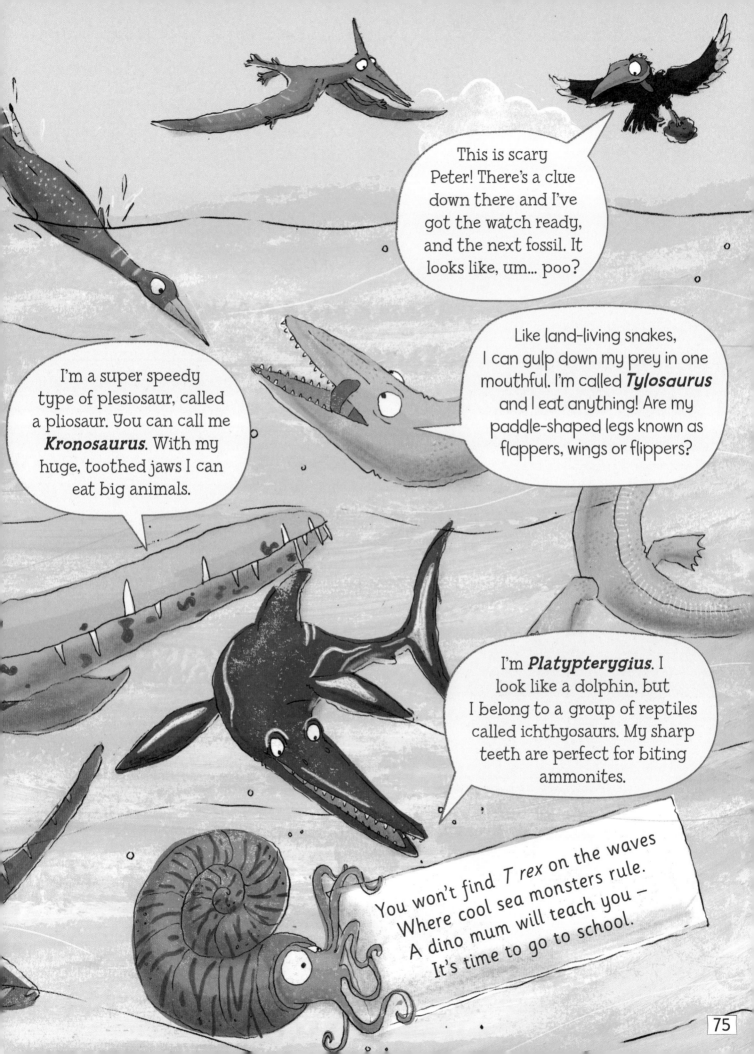

79

Pterodactylus

Ha ha – Peter went on a journey through time to find a dinosaur, but he had one with him all along!

That's called **evolution** and today's birds all evolved from dinosaurs.

Triceratops

Sinosauropteryx

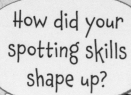

You've been on an adventure,
Meeting creatures on the way,
Tick the boxes if you saw them,
When you finish, shout "Hooray!"

Placerias ☐

Riojasaurus ☐

Melanorosaurus ☐

Postosuchus ☐

Giant dicynodont ☐

Triadobatrachus ☐

Archaeolepis mane ☐

Scelidosaurus ☐

Baryonyx ☐

Iguanodon ☐

Microraptor ☐

Hesperornis ☐

Pteranodon ☐

Ammonite ☐

Stygimoloch ☐

Stegoceras ☐

Acanthisitta ☐

Quetzalcoatlus ☐

Velociraptor ☐

Ichthyornis ☐

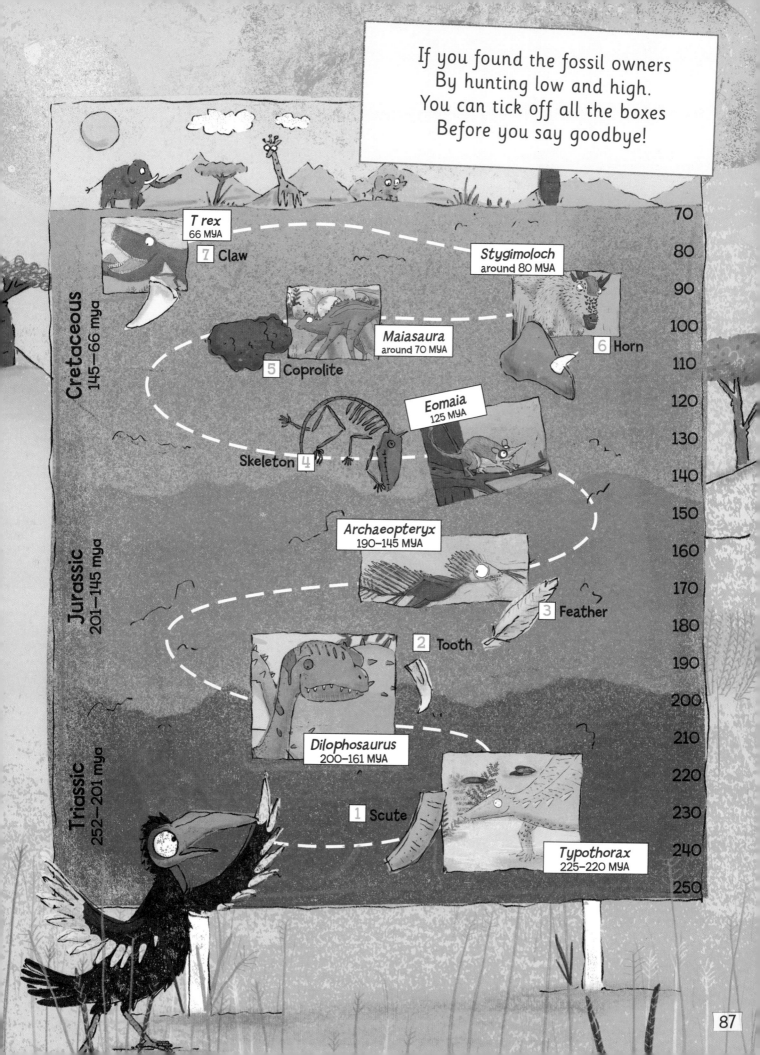

Hello!
I'm Molly.
I'm trying to spot all the bugs on this list so I can win my school's big bug hunt. Will you help me?
The Huge Bug Hunt
I'm Morpho. It would be easier for you to get close to bugs if you were a bit smaller. Some bugs are beautiful – unlike me.

89

Everyone in a termite mound is busy. They all have different jobs to do.

Find a way through the tunnel maze to the queen termite's nest – she'll tell you where to go next.

A termite mound can be more than 5 metres tall – all made of mud and dead plants glued together with spit! Use a measuring tape to find out how tall that is.

Those butterflies sprinkled magic dust on you, Molly! Now you're the right size to enter a termite mound.

I'm a **soldier termite** and I'm defending our nest from predators.

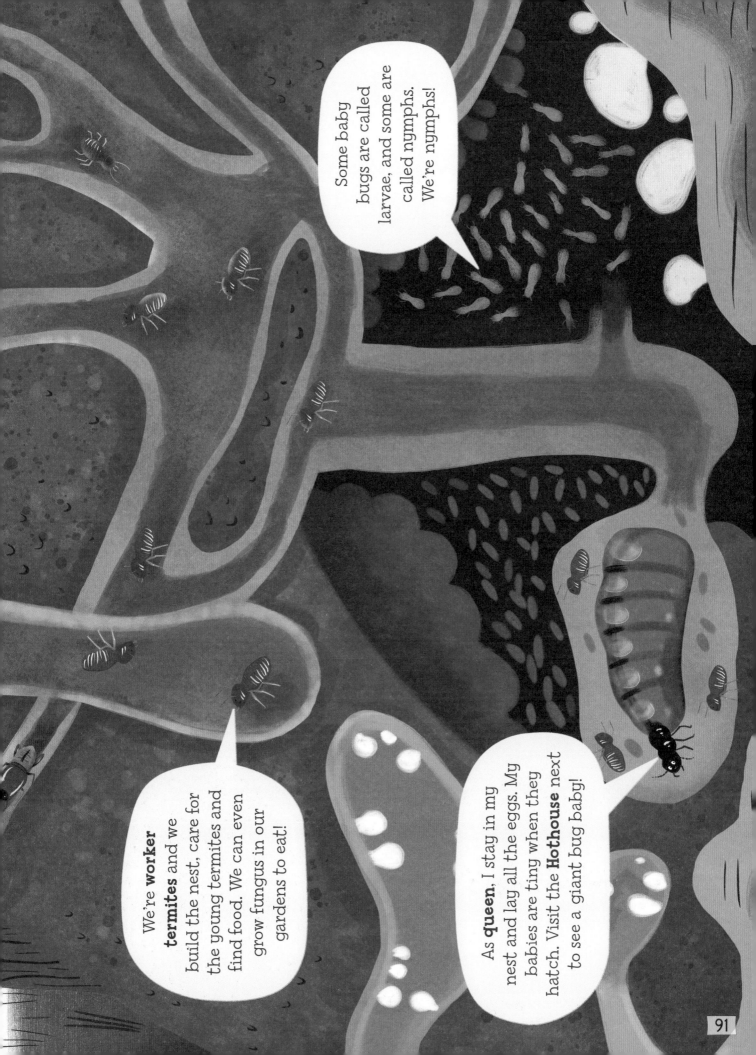

Some baby bugs are called larvae, and some are called nymphs. We're nymphs!

We're **worker termites** and we build the nest, care for the young termites and find food. We can even grow fungus in our gardens to eat!

As **queen**, I stay in my nest and lay all the eggs. My babies are tiny when they hatch. Visit the **Hothouse** next to see a giant bug baby!

It's so hot – and all these bugs are huge! Let's find the ones on the checklist fast, and get out of here!

The longest adult bug knows where you should go. I'm a **colossal earwig** and I'm as long as a child's finger.

I'm a **wind spider**, and I can run at up to 50 centimetres a second. My body is 7 centimetres long. Go to **Web World** next.

I'm an **Actaeon beetle** larva – a giant baby bug! I weigh as much as three apples.

I'm an adult **Actaeon beetle** from the Amazon Rainforest. I'm almost twice as long as the wind spider. Go to the Bed Bug Experience.

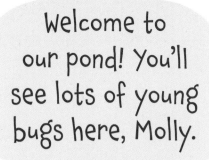

Welcome to our pond! You'll see lots of young bugs here, Molly.

Many baby bugs look and act very different to the adults they will become.

Unscramble the letters to find the name of each type of baby here. I'm an amphibian, not a bug. One day I'll be a frog!
p o d t a l e

I hang from the surface to breathe air – through my bottom! When I grow up I'll be a blood-sucking mosquito.
a r v l a

I'm sometimes called a baby dragon because when I grow up I'll be a dragonfly. What am I?
m y n p h

I'm a baby stickleback fish. Soon I'll grow spines on my back and hunt tadpoles! What are baby fish called?
r y f

94

95

I'm called a **net-casting spider** because I make a net from silk and throw it over my prey. Time to catch a grasshopper!

Yikes! I'm getting out of here... follow me Molly!

Bloody-nosed beetles like me make a foul red liquid when anyone gets too close. It looks scary and tastes bad.

Oh dear, the instructions for making bug masks have got muddled up. Can you work out the correct order?

Cut eyeholes and decorate your masks with paint to look like bug faces.

Blow up a balloon and tie it with string.

Hang the balloon so it can dry.

Dip the strips of torn paper into your glue and cover the balloon with them. Build up several layers of paper.

Use a pin to pop the balloon and ask an adult to cut the dried paper in half lengthways to make two masks.

Nom nom nom, yummy leaves, nom nom nom, yummy leaves...

We collect flower pollen and nectar to eat. In the hive we turn the nectar into honey. Is nectar a sugary liquid or a perfume?

Bugs move flowers' pollen around. This is called pollination, and it helps plants to grow.

I'm a **bumblebee** and I also visit flowers to suck the nectar, but I don't live in a hive.

Use the key in the hive cells to break this code and help Molly and Morpho find their next location:
41735172

105

I'm green so I'm camouflaged on a leaf. When a bug comes close I grab it in my claws and gobble it up. I'm a **praying mantis**.

Patterns and colours that blend with the surroundings are called camouflage. I'm a **leaf insect** – can you find any others like me?

I'm a **glasswing butterfly**. My wings are transparent. Does that mean that they are striped or see-through?

A **flower mantis** like me is perfectly camouflaged to disappear amongst the petals of a beautiful orchid.

Not all bugs are secretive,
Some are out to scare.
Fly off to the danger zone
And enter if you dare.

DANGER ZONE!
Some bugs use bright colours and patterns to warn other animals that they may be dangerous.

I'm going to keep a safe distance – just in case!

I flash the eye-spots on my wings. Predators think they are the real eyes of big animals and leave me alone.

I'm an **assassin bug.** I stab my victims with my sharp mouthparts and inject poison. Is it called denim or venom?

Am I a ladybird, or a spider pretending to be a ladybird?

Some animals look like other animals that are more dangerous than them. I'm a harmless **hoverfly.** What do I remind you of?

108

Molly is so tired after her huge bug hunt that she has fallen asleep. But where is Morpho?

Adult butterflies lay their eggs on the underside of leaves, to hide them from predators.

When they hatch, little caterpillars come out. They eat leaves and grow bigger.

I can eat half my body weight every day. That's like a child eating 20 lettuces!

Caterpillars getting ready to change spin a silken case around their body. The case is called a pupa and it turns hard.

An amazing change takes place inside a pupa. It's called a metamorphosis.

How many words can you make from the letters in METAMORPHOSIS?

A monarch butterfly spends four days as an egg, 14 as a caterpillar and 10 in a pupa. How many days is that altogether?
4 + 14 + 10 =

Butterflies have two long feelers on their heads called antennae. They use them to touch, smell, hear and taste.

Our wings are covered in lots of tiny colourful scales. They reflect light, so butterfly wings can shimmer and dazzle.

Butterflies and moths suck nectar from flowers, but some suck liquid from rotting fruit or meat too!

...emerge from his pupa! Now he's a beautiful big, blue butterfly!

Remember me? I'm called the **Queen Alexandra's birdwing** and I'm the biggest butterfly in the world!

I've had a lovely time on our journey Molly, and I've learned so much about my bug friends – we are all amazing!

You've been on an adventure,
You met creatures on the way,
Tick the boxes if you saw them,
When you've finished, shout "Hooray!"

Ladybird

Yellow slug

Lonomia caterpillar

Froghopper nymph

Large striped swordtail butterfly

Marsh fritillary butterfly

Sulphur butterfly

Velvet ant

Dragonfly nymph

Thorn bug

Dragonfly

Diving beetle

Mosquito

Cinnabar moth caterpillar

Cicada

Purple emperor butterfly

Woodlouse

Grasshopper

Cat flea

Dung beetle

Garden snail

Tiger moth

Tiger beetle

Rhinoceros cockroach

Queen Alexandra's birdwing butterfly

Stink bug

Merveille du Jour moth

Swallowtail butterfly

Crab spider

Ladybird spider

Glow beetle

Owl butterfly

Apollo butterfly

Elephant hawk moth

Leafcutter bee

Money spider

House spider

Leafcutter ant

Queen Alexandra's birdwing butterfly caterpillar

Hercules beetle

Peacock butterfly

Giant water snail

BUG KINGDOM

Web World

1 Butterfly House

2 Termite Town

10 Danger Zone

9 Secret City

3 Hothouse

4 Paradise Pond

8 Farmyard

6 Activity Centre

5 Tree Trail

7 Honey House

Bed Bug Experience

You've been on a big bug hunt
And recorded what you've seen.
Now your super search is over,
Can you tick off where you've been?

Hi! We're a **constellation** – a collection of stars! We're called **Gemini**, which means 'twins'.

Hoo-who's there?

Oh, it's you, Leo – gazing through your telescope, as usual. What would you want to look at most if you could go into space?

THE SPEEDY SPACE CHASE

I'd love to see a shooting star up close. Look, Stella – there's one there now! I wish I knew what they are and where they come from.

I'm another **constellation**. My name is **Taurus**, meaning 'bull'. I contain two bright clusters of stars.

Let's make a wish upon the shooting star. If only we had a real spaceship we could chase it...

Two pals spot a shooting star that's far from planet earth. To find out more about it, let's learn about its birth.

Wow – I never thought wishing on a star would actually work!

I'll program the computer to take us to OUR star – the Sun. Maybe it will shine a light on any nearby shooting stars.

You need a powerful rocket to get into space. Is the force that pulls things towards Earth's centre called gravity or gravy?

I'm a **griffin vulture** – one of the few birds that can fly as high as a plane. The layer of air around Earth is called the atmosphere. It contains oxygen – the gas that you and I breathe.

Hello there – I don't get many visitors! I'm the **Sun** and I am a burning ball of gases. I am 330,000 times bigger than Earth and I make heat and light.

Hi, I'm **Mercury**, the closest planet to the Sun. Come and visit me!

Solar flares are bursts of energy that blaze on the Sun's surface. What word is used for things to do with the Sun?
a. Solar b. Sofar c. Sonar

My readings all spell danger, this heat is much too strong. We'll just touch down on Mercury, we really can't stay long.

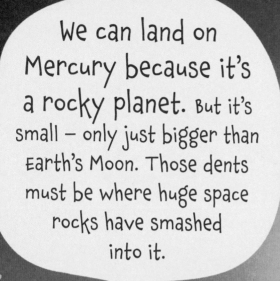

We can land on Mercury because it's a rocky planet. But it's small — only just bigger than Earth's Moon. Those dents must be where huge space rocks have smashed into it.

The dents are called craters. This giant one is called the Caloris Basin. It formed when a massive space rock (we call them asteroids) hit Mercury nearly 4 billion years ago. Does a billion have 5 zeros or 9 zeros?

I'm **Messenger**, the first spacecraft to fly all around Mercury. When I finished studying the planet I crashed onto its surface.

Hello – you know me! I'm **EARTH**, and I'm a pretty perfect place to live.

I have air and water – two of the essential things for life to thrive.

Earth takes 365 days – one year – to travel around the Sun. That journey is called an orbit.

Earth is not too hot and not too cold – Mercury and Venus are both! So far, Earth is the only place in the whole Universe where there is life.

I'm Earth's closest neighbour, but I'm not a planet. There are eight planets in our Solar System, and Earth is the third planet from the Sun. Can you learn all the other planets' names?

A shooting star may have brought the first water to Earth. Today only about one quarter of Earth's surface isn't underwater. Come and dock with us to find out more!

As it orbits, Earth spins on its axis once every 24 hours. It's daytime on the side facing the Sun, and night time on the side facing away.

127

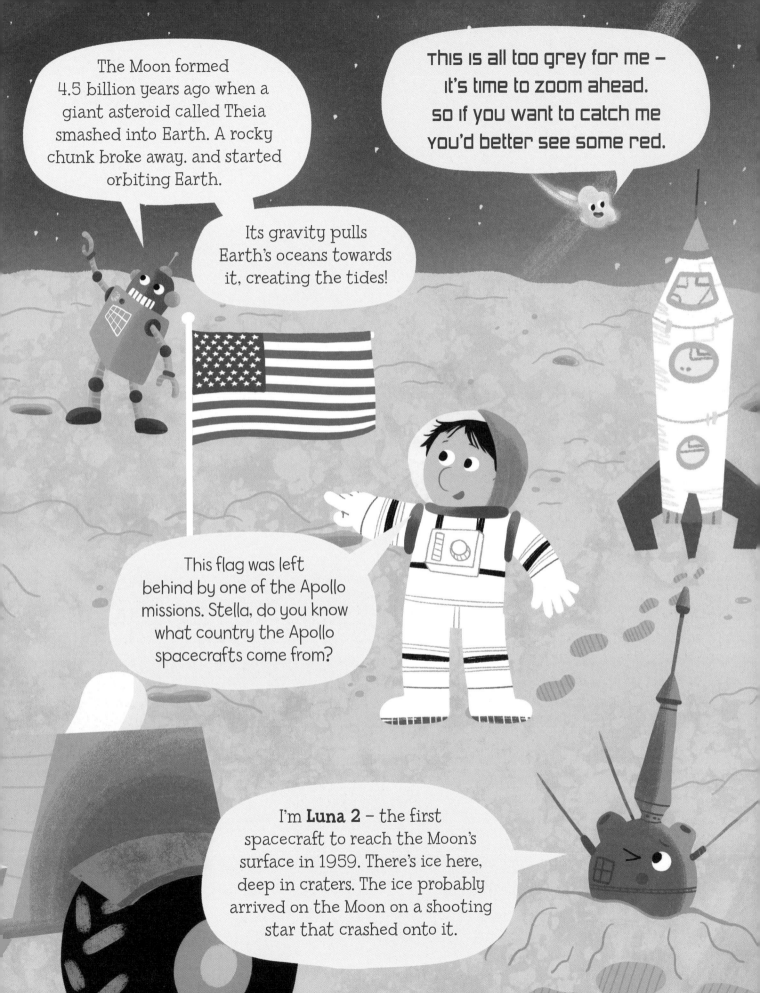

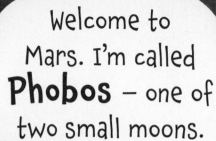

Welcome to Mars. I'm called **Phobos** – one of two small moons.

You are the first living things to walk on Mars, but maybe some form of life lived here long ago – no one knows!

I can jump up 50 centimetres on Earth, but here on Mars the gravity is so weak I can jump three times higher. How high is that?

My name is **Curiosity**, and I'm a **rover** – a type of robot. I'm using my arm to collect rocks, soil and to look for signs of life.

Mars is called the Red Planet because it is covered in red rocks and sand. I'm a rover too. I stopped working in 2018 after I got smothered by a dust storm. Look out... another one is coming!

Did you know that Mars has icy poles like Earth, and some liquid water?

I'm an enormous volcano called **Olympus Mons**, and I'm three times bigger than Mount Everest on your planet.

Leo, there's a huge dust storm coming our way. Let's get out of here!

Brrr. it's much colder here than on Earth! That's because we've been moving further away from the Sun.

oh no – you've reached the asteroid belt! To find a safe path from Mars to Jupiter, work out whether each statement is true or false. Correct answers will keep you on track.

START

Oh dear! Mars really is red. The red comes from a mineral called iron oxide.

F

T

Venus is the second planet from the Sun.

Nope! It is known as the Big Bang.

T

The beginning of the Universe was called the Big Snap.

F

F

Gravity is a force that pushes.

T

T

The fifth planet from the Sun is made of gas.

F

Sorry, the fifth planet is Jupiter and it's definitely made of gas.

If an asteroid breaks up, the pieces are called meteors. If they fly through Earth's atmosphere they will burn, and make one type of shooting star – a meteorite!

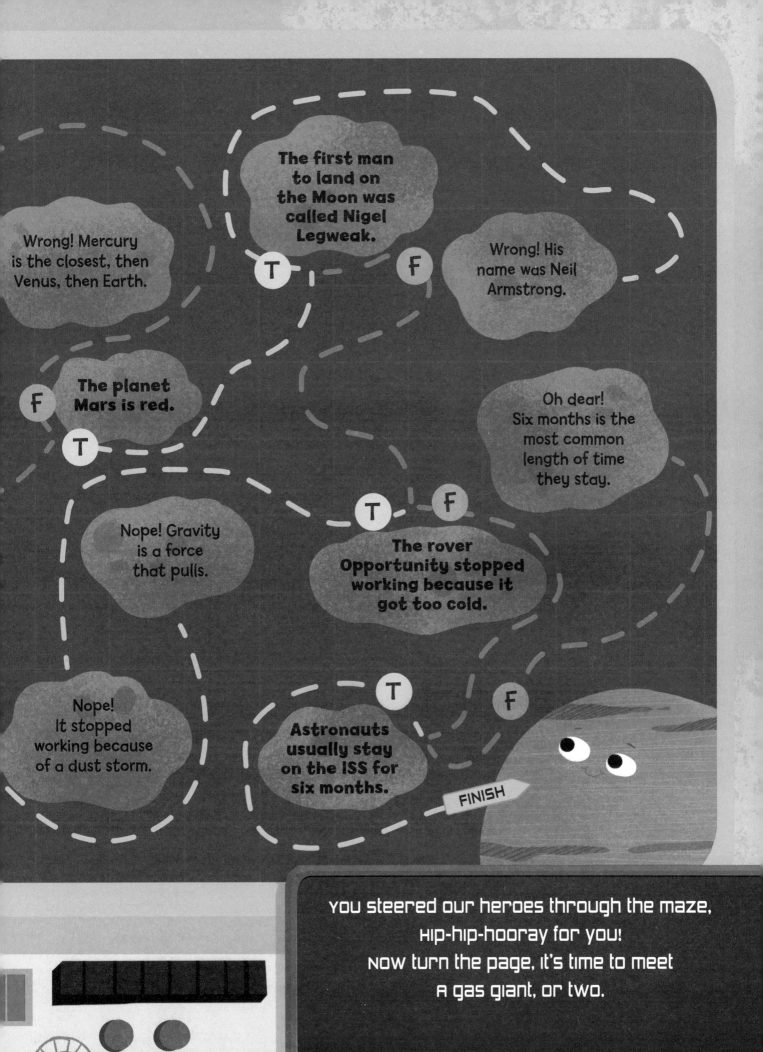

Wow, Stella – you did a great job of steering the spacecraft through the Asteroid Belt.

I'm **Jupiter**, the largest planet in the Solar System. You've landed on Io, one of my many moons.

There are volcanoes everywhere – but at least Io is made of solid rock! Jupiter doesn't have any 'land' to land on – just swirling gases with huge storms whipping around its surface.

My name is **Europa**, and the ice sheet that covers me is up to 25 kilometres thick. Underneath it are huge oceans full of water, which might contain life! You'll have to come and visit me one day to find out.

I can see one of your giant storms, Jupiter – the Red Spot. I read it's a hurricane twice as big as Earth that has been raging for a century. How many years is that – 10 or 100?

I'm an orbiter called **Juno** and I left Earth in 2011. I'm now orbiting Jupiter to find out how it formed, if it has water, and to study its huge storms.

Jupiter has more than 75 moons. I'm **Ganymede** – the biggest. What word describes the shape of planets and moons? If you think it's 'sphere' fly towards Saturn, but if you think it's 'cube' head straight for Pluto.

Jupiter's four biggest moons were discovered by the great scientist Galileo Galilei. My name is **Callisto**. Unscramble the letters to discover what Galileo used to see us:
C-O-P-E-S-L-E-E-T

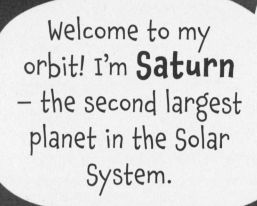

Welcome to my orbit! I'm **Saturn** – the second largest planet in the Solar System.

One year on me lasts nearly 30 Earth years. Five spacecraft have visited me but nothing can land because I'm made of gas, like Jupiter. I have over 50 moons. How many can you see?

Saturn spins faster than Earth and one day has less than 11 hours. How many hours are in one Earth day?

Don't get too close! Saturn's sky has incredible lightning and thunderstorms. They go on for months with 10 bright flashes every single second.

I'm **Titan**. and it's not safe to land on me either. I have lakes and oceans, but they are full of deadly chemicals. Raindrops on me are as big as marbles.

This is so exciting – we were chasing a shooting star and now we're riding on it!

We're right at the far edges of the Solar System. Look there's Neptune – the final planet.

I was launched to explore the Kuiper Belt. Some shooting stars are meteorites and some of them are comets. Comets came from the Big Bang, when the Universe began.

I'm headed back towards Earth, so I'll take you home. I'm a comet – a giant snowball of ice and gas that orbits the Sun. People often call comets shooting stars. I formed beyond the Kuiper Belt, in a place called the Oort Cloud.

My name is **Neptune**, and I'm a dark, cold, windy ice giant. It takes me 165 Earth years to orbit the Sun, and I'm 4.5 billion kilometres away from it. Can you see my faint rings?

We're icy bits of rock and ice, comets and dwarf planets. We make a ring beyond Neptune called the Kuiper Belt, so we're called **KBOs** or **Kuiper Belt Objects**.

I'm **Pluto** and I'm in the Kuiper Belt too. My big moon is called Charon.

Pluto was the ninth planet in the Solar System, but it was decided that he was too small. Now people say he's a 'dwarf planet' instead. He's not too happy about it!

We liked meeting other planets on our speedy chase through space, but I think the biggest lesson is that earth's a precious place!

How did your spotting skills shape up?

You've been on an adventure,
Spotting things along the way,
Tick their boxes if you saw them,
When you're finished, shout "Hooray!"

Thebe ☐	Optical telescope ☐	Elara ☐	Solar flare ☐
Deimos ☐	Neptune ☐	Apollo Lunar Roving Vehicle ☐	Uranus ☐
Amalthea ☐	High-level cloud ☐	Enceladus ☐	Constellation of Orion ☐
Crew Dragon ☐	Saturn ☐	Spacewalking astronaut ☐	Makemake ☐
Earth ☐	Airbus 350 plane ☐	Mars ☐	New Horizons ☐
The Great Red Spot ☐	Charon ☐	Opportunity rover ☐	Jupiter ☐
Mercury ☐	Constellation of Leo ☐	Venus ☐	Akatsuki space probe ☐